George Duncan Gibb

Odd Showers

An Explanation of the Rain of Insects, Fishes, and Lizards

George Duncan Gibb

Odd Showers
An Explanation of the Rain of Insects, Fishes, and Lizards

ISBN/EAN: 9783744692625

Printed in Europe, USA, Canada, Australia, Japan

Cover: Foto ©ninafisch / pixelio.de

More available books at **www.hansebooks.com**

ODD SHOWERS:

OR,

AN EXPLANATION OF THE RAIN

OF

Insects, Fishes, and Lizards; Soot, Sa̶̶̶̶shes;
Red Rain and Snow; Meteoric̶
and other Bodies.

BY

CARRIBBE̶

INTENDED CHIEFLY FOR YO̶

LONDON:
KERBY & SON, 190, OXFORD
1870.

TO

MY DAUGHTER,

RICARDA CECILIA,

THESE PAGES

ARE AFFECTIONATELY

Inscribed.

London, *October*, 1870.

ODD SHOWERS.

My attention was first directed to the subject of "Odd Showers" on Sunday, 25th July, 1841, when riding on horseback with a relative from the village of St. Henri, known as "The Tanneries," to the St. Pierre Race Course, on the Island of Montreal, in Canada. Shortly after crossing the bridge over the canal, our attention was attracted to myriads of little things hopping across the road in all directions, which we recognized to be small frogs. I dismounted and collected a lot of them in my pocket handkerchief, which was replaced in my pocket; and it was the impression of my friend and myself at the time, that the multitude of these little creatures observed within a limited space, say about half-a-mile along the road, must have been the result of a shower, a view which was favoured by the occurrence of a smart rain just before we came up, for the ground was quite wet. This was about half-past two or three o'clock in the afternoon of a beautiful summer's day. There was meadow land on each side of the road, and no stream of water for a considerable distance, and we took it for granted there had been a shower of frogs. This was one of those popular errors in which we as well as others before us had been mistaken, and which has been perpetuated since the time of Pliny. Nevertheless it induced me from that time to lose no opportunity of acquiring information concerning the "Odd Showers" of both living and dead substances with which various parts of the earth are favoured every now and then ; and as a number of materials accumulated in my hands during the period that has elapsed—29 years—since our encounter with the frogs, they have been sifted to the best advantage and embodied in this little work, which has no other pretentions beyond attracting attention to a curious and interesting corner in the domain of physical science.

Before proceeding further a word about the frogs. On our return to the City of Montreal, they were for the time forgotten, until painfully and awkwardly brought to remembrance. Whilst taking tea with the company (which included several ladies,) in the drawing room at my relative's house, my frogs escaped out of the folds of my handkerchief and popped out of my pocket on to the floor. Not content with that they hopped on to the legs of the ladies who were seated around the table, and in a few minutes, this was followed by screaming and jumping up, when the mystery was quickly solved. All assisted to capture the reptiles which are now preserved in the Museum of the Natural History Society at Montreal.

Although the rain of frogs is one of those popular errors that is widely prevalent, yet it must be stated that a *shower* of these creatures, is within the range of possibility, equally so with fishes and lizards, illustrated farther on, if any stream or pool of water containing them was sucked up by a waterspout or otherwise raised by a hurricane and transported to a distance more or less remote.

In considering the subject, it will be convenient to take those "Odd Showers" first wherein living things have rained, and then the various substances devoid of animal life. Those bodies which are presumed to have come from regions beyond our globe, shall come last.

SHOWERS OF INSECTS.

In our temperate climate insects have not been known in recent times to exist in such abundance as to constitute showers. An exception, perhaps, might be made in favour of *Ephemerae*, which have been seen to fill the air for miles on the banks of the streams in the Midland Counties, dropping towards the surface of the ground or water, like fine drops of rain ; or as Reaumur has described it from observation on the banks of the Marne and Seine, "When the snow falls with the largest flakes and with the least interval between them, the air is not so filled as it was around me with ephemerae : scarcely had I remained in one place a few minutes when the step on which I stood was quite concealed with a layer of them, from 2 to 4 inches in depth." The water near was thickly covered with them, and as they fell obliquely, the eyes, mouth, and nostrils were filled. These insect showers are welcomed by fishermen as the forerunners of abundance.

I have seen the same thing occur in Canada in the months of May and June, generally May, along the banks of the St. Lawrence, where the Shad-fly (an ephemeral insect) comes as an annual visitor in countless swarms in most of the villages and towns on each side of that noble river as far up as Montreal, during the time that the shad-fish is tracing its course upwards to deposit its spawn. The fish at this period is caught in large numbers; the shad-fly forms the principal food of the fish, and on its first appearance the markets are generally well supplied with the latter. The quantity of these flies in the air resembles a heavy fall of snow, and everything is filled by them. On the banks of the St. Lawrence as far as the eye can reach, the air is filled with falling flies, as if they came from the clouds. Fortunately they are harmless, and do not last longer than from two to three days in any one locality. The question is asked, Where do they come from?

They are hatched simultaneously in millions from the pupa and aquatic larvae of the parent insects in all the streams and rivers, for probably an extent of many hundred miles on the banks of the St. Lawrence.

Showers of *Phryganeae* (Caddice-flies) occur in some parts of the continent of Europe, not unlike those of the ephemerae, when the air is said to be filled for a considerable distance. As travellers well know to their misfortune, *Mosquitoes* exist in some countries in numbers that baffle description, and their blood-thirsty habits induce them to attack one in countless myriads. They rain perhaps in equal, but not greater number than the ephemerae and their allies. The *Gnats* are just as bad. The larvae of these insects are aquatic, and abound in stagnant water, but it is doubtful whether they ever exist in such numbers as the ephemerae, although perfect pests to human kind.

In insect showers all must yield precedence to the *Locusts*. Clouds of these, according to the accounts of various travellers, are often so dense and extensive as to obscure the sun in such countries as the East, various parts of Africa, Tartary, Russia, and Poland.

Their occurrence is easily explained : swarms of these insects appear in a certain locality, deposit their eggs, which soon come to maturity, and the larvae march onwards, eat up and devastate everything before them. In three or four weeks they are metamorphosed into the perfect insect, and mount in millions. Africa has been ravaged by them from time immemorial, and Holy Writ bears evidence of the miseries they have produced. In 1797 Barrow observed them in South Africa in swarms, covering the country for an extent of 2000 miles. Vast clouds frequently appear in Tartary, and extend westward into Poland and Russia.

Clouds of *Ants* are sometimes seen in Europe in August or September, just emerged from the pupa state. They have been compared to columns of vapour as they rise in the air or change their position, twisting and whirling about in various directions.

Of living showers, insects are unquestionably the most abundant, from the reasons which have been given ; it is not so with other things. If fish or other bodies rain, it is from some unusual and peculiar circumstance, as shall now be shown.

SHOWERS OF FISHES.

Several well authenticated accounts of showers of fish have been placed on record, and now-a-days the natural philosopher does not doubt the actual descent of the fish, but that they should rain from the clouds. It is abundantly evident that, even assuming the fish to be carried upwards by means of a waterspout or whirlwind, they could not live for any length of time, and must soon descend by the natural laws of gravitation, when the forces that elevated them were spent. A few examples will suffice in illustration.

On Wednesday before Easter in 1666, a pasture field of two acres, at Cranstead, near Wrotham, in Kent, was all overspread with little fishes, supposed to have rained down, as there was at the time a great tempest of thunder and rain. Wrotham is far from the sea, there were no fish-ponds near, but a great scarcity of water. The fish were of the length of the little finger, and proved to be young whitings, and the quantity was estimated to be about a bushel; none were found in any adjoining fields. This account was given in a letter from Dr. Robert Conny, to the late Dr. Robert Plot, F.R.S., who it seems had promised the former an account of a shower of herrings. *(Phil. Tran.* vol. 20, p. 289.)

My friend, Dr. Arthur Fisher, drew my attention to a shower of pilchards he had read of. A shower of live fish occurred at Benares in India, in July, 1860, unaccompanied by rain. A similar shower, but accompanied by rain fell some years before at Agra. These were noticed in the local papers, and are referred to in the letter from the Deputy Commissioner, Dhurmsalla to E. H. Davies, Esq. Secretary to the Government, Punjab. To take an instance at home which was published in *The Times* of February 25th, 1859, by the Rev. Aaron Roberts, B.A., Curate of St. Peter's, Caermarthen. His account was that "On Friday, the 11th of February, there fell at Mountain Ash, Glamorganshire, about 9 o'clock a.m. in and about the premises of Mr. Nixon, a heavy shower of rain and small fish. The largest size measured about four inches in length. It is supposed that two different species of fish descended; on this point, however, the public generally disagree. At the

time it was blowing a very stiff gale from the South.
Several of the fish are preserved in fresh water,
five of which I have this day seen. They seem to
thrive well. The tail and fins are of a bright white
colour. Some persons attempting to preserve a few
in salt and water, the effect is stated to have been
almost instantaneous death. It was not observed at
the time that any fish fell in any other part of the
neighbourhood, save in the particular spot mentioned.
Appended is a paragraph on the case taken out of the
Monmouthshire Merlin :

"SHOWER OF FISH.—Much excitement has been
occasioned in the valley of Aberdare by the fact of
a complete shower of fish falling at Mountain Ash, on
Friday last. The roofs of some houses were covered
with them, and several were living, and are still preserved in life and apparent health in glass bottles.
They were from an inch to three inches in length,
and fell during a heavy shower of rain and storm
of wind."

The foregoing is intentionally given unabridged,
and as the fish fell in a living state it is quite clear,
that they must have left their place of abode but a

very short time before, which may have been fresh
water, as they immediately died in artificial sea
water, although this is by no means conclusive.
Their tumbling in a heavy shower of rain, together
with their comparatively small size, would favor the
opinion that they may have been included in the
column of a waterspout drawn upwards, which as it
disseminated in vapour, was as quickly followed by a
heavy shower, in which the fish descended.

> —————"The dreadful spout,
> Which shipmen do the hurricano call,
> Constring'd in mass by the almighty sun."
>
> SHAKESPEARE *(Troilus and Cressida.)*

Their tumbling upon the roofs of several houses at
a period of the day when anything unusual would
have been noticed, favors the view that a hurricane
did not drive them from their natural place of abode.
The distance of the valley of Aberdare from the sea,
southwards, is about twenty miles.

That isolated showers of fish have happened in
various localities, the result of atmospheric disturbances, the evidence furnished is too clear to admit a
doubt of. When once elevated, from whatever cause,

the propelling force and velocity of the wind would
prove sufficient to carry them a considerable distance
—say many miles—before the laws of gravitation
would begin to exert themselves. Showers of fish
are not more extraordinary than the *ejection of fish
from volcanoes*, a circumstance which has occurred
near Quito, where liquid mud ejected by the volcanoes often involves myriads of small dead fish.
Pimelodes Cyclopum. (Cyc. Brit. ed. 8, vol. 3, p. 129.)

SHOWERS OF LIZARDS.

The great abundance of fish compared with the
scarcity of lizards necessarily invests a shower of the
latter with considerable interest, and the instance
here given is the only one that has come under
my notice. A newspaper extract from the *Montreal
Weekly Gazette* of 28th December, 1857, furnished
the following :—

"SHOWER OF LIZARDS.—The Leroy (N.Y.) *Gazette*
says that, during the heavy rain of Sunday night last,
live lizards, some of them measuring four inches in

length, fell from the clouds like manna, though not as plentiful, nor half so welcome. They were found crawling on the side walks and in the streets, like infantile fugitive alligators in places far removed from localities where they inhabit."

If this account is reliable, then the lizard here mentioned must be the yellow bellied water newt, which exists in abundance in some of the waters and streams of the North American rivers, especially in the State of New York, Canada, and neighbouring places. I have caught these lizards with greater ease and in larger numbers than fish in particular localities, and providing that they have existed in number sufficient, the only possible mode of explanation of a shower of them, is that by which the fish, already referred to, were taken up into the clouds, namely, by means of a land waterspout, or possibly carried onwards by a hurricane. In North America tornadoes and whirlwinds are by no means uncommon, and occur at various intervals of time. Those who object to this theory must be prepared with a better one, to account for the presence of lizards on the side walks and streets of a small town.

They are not animals that leave the water and crawl over land like small frogs. Their presence on the roofs of the houses would not have strengthened the argument for or against their being due to a shower. A reference to the map of the State of New York, shows Leroy to be twenty-three miles south of Lake Ontario, or twenty south-west of the City of Rochester. It lays at the foot of a hill, and in front runs a stream, and another a few miles to the north, both of them tributaries of the Genessee River, twelve miles to the east. Some one of these waters was, doubtless, the source whence the lizards were transferred to the spot already mentioned, through the agency of a waterspout.

SHOWERS OF SOOT, SAND, AND ASHES.

I bind the sun's throne with a burning zone,
And the moon's with a girdle of pearl ;
The volcanoes are dim, and the stars reel and swim,
When the whirlwinds my banner unfurl.

Shelley.

As these substances are chiefly the product of volcanic eruptions, they shall be considered together. The heavy scoriae that are ejected in small fragments from any volcano, do not become propelled to any great distance, unless from constant attrition they become reduced to the form of ashes or fine sand. Under these circumstances currents of air will transport them to considerable distances, amounting sometimes to hundreds of miles, although apparently opposed by the direct course of the wind. According to their degree of consistence and fineness, the ejecta of volcanoes receive various names from the

Italian geologists : thus, *lapillo* signifies a fine frag-
mentary gravel or rounded scoriae, of a deep black
colour ; if the attrition is carried still further it con-
stitutes the red *puzzolana*, resembling burnt brick
dust ; and if finally converted into a condition of
fine dust, of a whitish grey, it forms *ceneri* or ashes
(Scrope). Although this division holds good, not
unfrequently the three varieties are intermixed, but
sometimes include fragments of other rocks which
have been produced by former eruptions.

An unusual circumstance is a shower of black
dust or ashes, so fine as to resemble *soot*. This
occurred at Montreal in Canada, on two successive
days in 1819, and attracted much attention in
Europe. On November 8th, dense black clouds let
fall a heavy shower of rain, depositing a substance,
which, to the eye, the taste, and the smell, presented
the appearance of common soot. Next day, at noon,
the darkness was extreme, from clouds described as
almost pitchy black ; this was followed in three
hours by thunder, lightning, and rain, and a shock
of an earthquake. The rain deposited larger quan-
tities of soot than on the previous day, and as it

flowed through the streets it carried on its surface a dense foam resembling soap suds. The range of this phenomenon extended to below Quebec, above Kingston, and in many parts of the United States. The source of the soot was never accurately traced, but in all probability it was from some far distant volcano. This is by no means surprising when we recollect that the volcanic dust, reduced to an impalpable powder, that was ejected in the frightful volcanic eruption in Sumbawa, in 1815 (200 miles from the eastern extremity of Java), was carried through the upper regions of the atmosphere to the islands of Amboyna and Banda, the last 800 miles east of the volcano. The darkness occasioned in the day time by the ashes, in Java, was so profound that it equalled the darkest night known (Lyell.) A great fall of black dust fell near Con-stantinople, in 472, during which the heavens seemed to burn. A black dust like lampblack fell in Shetland, in October, 1755, which smelt strongly of sulphur, covered the faces and hands and blackened the linen of the people in the fields. As the wind was S.W. it was presumed to be from Hecla, 500 and 600 miles further north *(Phil. Tran.)* This I think is undoubtedly true.

A shower of *red dust* is mentioned by Theophrastus as occurring at Constantinople in 652; and Quatremère refers to a fall of red sand from a red sky at Bagdad in 929. Kaswini describes red dust and matter like coagulated blood that fell from the heavens in the middle of the ninth century. An account is given by Valisnieri of red dust that fell in 1689, at Venice and other places. At the end of September, 1815, the South Sea was covered to a great extent with dust, supposed to have proceeded from the fall of a meteor *(Phil. Mag.)* but which I believe to have originated from a neighbouring volcano.

From the repeated projection upwards of fragments of stones and lapilli, and their fall back again into craters, they undergo such an amount of trituration as to be reduced to a condition of sand and fine ashes, which finally are carried upwards, and form clouds which extend to great distances, according to the currents of wind then prevailing. In the eighth century darkness prevailed in the volcanic mountains of Armenia, during forty days, from immense clouds of volcanic ashes. Great as these showers must have been, they are slight in comparison with those of the volcano of Guayta-Putina, near Arequipa in Peru, in February, 1600, which for twenty continuous days vomited such a quantity of stones, sand, and ashes, that the showers covered the surrounding country to a distance of ninety miles on one side, and 120 on the other. The great' eruption of Vesuvius in the year 79, buried Herculaneum, Pompeii, and Stabiae, with its showers of ashes and other ejecta. In 472, according to Procopius, an eruption of Vesuvius occurred, which covered all Europe with ashes. In 1812 ashes fell from a great height in the atmosphere upon Barbadoes, in great profusion, which had been projected from the volcano in the island of St. Vincent. In January, 1835, the volcano of Cosequina, one of the Andes, was in eruption, and some of its ashes fell at Truxillo, on the shores of the Gulf of Mexico. The same shower of ashes fell at Kingston, Jamaica, having been carried by an upper counter current against the regular east wind, which was then blowing (Lyell). Kingston is 700 miles from Cosequina, and these ashes must have been more than four days in the air, having travelled 170 miles a day. Captain Badeley describes a rain of sand or ashes *(Phil. Tran.)* that began at ten p.m. on December 6th, 1631, when his ship was at anchor in the Gulf of Volo, and continued until two a.m. of next day; forming a layer two inches thick on the deck. A great shower of ashes occurred in the river St. Lawrence, July 3rd, 1814 *(Phil. Mag.)*

Instances of showers of dust, sand, and ashes, could be multiplied, but the foregoing are sufficient to illustrate the subject.

As relating to volcanic phenomena, may be mentioned a cretaceous grey rain, occurring near Mount Etna in 1781. A shower of mud, mingled with rain, fell heavily at three p.m. for upwards of twenty minutes, in the Straits of Messina, on March 23rd, 1869; the sky was very black, and the decks of the P. & O. C. Steamer resembled something like the London Streets after a sharp rain *(Scientific Opinion*, April 7th, 1869, p. 439). This was clearly a mixture of sand and ashes with rain, forming the mud.

SHOWERS OF SAND, NON-VOLCANIC.

Whilst examples have been given of showers of sand and ashes that owe their origin to volcanoes, a few words are necessary upon those of the first arising from deserts and arid sandy plains. Every one must be familiar with the account of the pillars of sand in the African deserts, and of the violent whirlwinds which prevail. When these last rage with irresistible force, accompanied by violent gusts of wind, they bear upwards immense bodies of sand, which in time subside, the heavier particles doing so completely, whilst the lighter form a sort of vapour, elevated a certain distance above the level of the sand waves. The following verse from Darwin expresses more than any description could give :—

SANDS OF THE DESERT.

Now o'er their head the whizzing whirlwinds breathe,
And the live desert pants and heaves beneath ;
Tinged by the crimson sun, vast columns rise
Of eddying sands, and war amid the skies ;
In red arcades the billowy plain surround,
And striking turrets dance upon the ground.

Veritable showers of the sands of these African deserts have rained upon the arable land of Egypt, on the western bank of the Nile, being blown by west winds through the valleys opening into the plain or gorges through the Libyan mountains. Many ruins of ancient cities in Egypt have been buried by sand drifts. Towns and villages have been entombed in England, France, and Jutland, by blown sand. In Northern Mexico, Froebel discovered on one occasion, the smoke of five fires in the distance, which proved to be columns of dust caused by whirlwinds. He describes the shifting sand of the Mexican desert of the Medanos, between limestone hills, bounded like a lake, but with a surface in waves like those of the ocean. The north of China is subject to singular showers of sand, which were first described by Dr. Macgowan.

SHOWERS OF RED RAIN AND RED SNOW, VEGETABLE AND OTHER ORGANISMS.

The so-called showers of blood of many of the older writers, at one time looked upon as a terrible and fatal omen, consisted of ordinary rain tinged or mixed with some red substances, generally of a vegetable nature, or of the red exudations of certain butterflies. Numerous instances of red rain and red snow are given by many of the older writers, and are by no means chimerical. To take a few chronologically:—According to Spangenberg, red rain fell in Bohemia in 1416. Showers of blood fell in several places in 1501, on the authority of different chronicles. Fromard mentions red rain falling at Embden, in Louvain, in 1560; and Count Natalis, a fiery meteor and red rain at Lillebonne, in the same year. Leman refers to a shower of blood at La Magdalaine, near Orleans, in 1591. A great fall of stones, with a shower of blood, occurred at Styria in 1618, as stated by De Hammer.

Red rain fell at Tournay in 1638; at Bois-le-Duc in January, and at Brussels in October, 1645; at Orsio, in Sweden, in May, 1711; at San Pietro d'Arena, near Genoa, in 1744; and in several countries in November, 1755; a red sky was associated with the red rain in the last. Mercurio describes red rain at Cleves, Utrecht, &c. in 1763; it occurred in Picardy, in November, 1765. I need scarcely observe that the causes of the redness in all these varies, and will be understood from what follows. During the atmospheric disturbances that occurred in India, in the early part of the year 1860, when several aerolites fell, portions of which were transmitted to this country, according to the official letter of the Deputy Commissioner at Dhurmsalla, to the Secretary of the Government, Punjab, dated 30th July, 1860, a "shower of blood" is mentioned as occurring at Furruckabad, and another at Meerut previously. An instance that occurred nearer home in the same year, and correctly termed *Red Rain*, falling at Sienna, was communicated to the French Acadamy in a letter from M. S. de Luca. The details are in *Comtes Rendus*, 21st January, 1861,

(p. 107.) On the 28th and 31st December, 1860, and 1st January, 1861, there fell in certain localities of the town of Sienna, a feebly coloured red rain, and on those days in the atmosphere was observed by some persons clouds of a reddish tint, and the snow that fell in some places was similarly coloured. M. Luca examined some of the collected rain, and clearly made out, microscopically and chemically, the colouring matter to be of an organic nature, probably of a species of plant belonging to the Algae, related to the *Hygrocrocis Cyclaminae*, which furnishes a rose solution. No great stretch of imagination is required to comprehend the generation of the vegetable or plant like organisms in the clouds, if the rising earth's vapour was charged with the necessary elements of growth and fecundation. And we have consequently a simple explanation of red rain or red snow according to circumstances. Crimson snow described by Captain Ross in his voyage to Baffins Bay, was supposed by Dr. Wollaston to owe its complexion to some vegetable production, this was confirmed by Mr. Bauer who discovered the existence of a nondescript *uredo*, which he designated *nivalis*.

In the beginning of July, 1608, a supposed shower of blood fell for several miles around the suburbs of Aix la Chapelle. The cause of this was discovered by M. de Peirese to depend upon the exudation of large drops of a blood coloured liquid on the transformation of large chrysalides into the butterfly state. The drops produced red stains on the walls of the small villages in the neighbourhood, on stones in the highways, and in the fields. The number of butterflies flying about too was prodigious. These red drops were not found in the middle of the city or in places where the butterflies did not reach. To the same cause M. de Pereise attributes (I think very correctly) some other showers of blood related by historians, that happened in the warm season of the year when butterflies are most numerous. Gregory of Tours, mentions one that fell in the time of Childebert in different parts of Paris, and upon a certain house in the territory of Senlis; and about the end of the month of June, another likewise fell in the reign of King Robert. Large drops of excrement of the colour of blood are voided by all the butterflies which proceed from the different species of hairy caterpillar. On one occasion twenty-eight chrysalides of *Vanessa antiopa*, or Camberwell beauty, which I had preserved in a small room, attached to projecting bodies, underwent transformation on a single day in July; the walls and floor were so bespattered with bright crimson-coloured fluid, resembling blood, as to give the appearance of a regular shower of the fluid.

Although showers of red rain have been well attested by the most reliable authorities, a writer in *Rees Cyclop.* (1819) has stated that they are by no means to be credited, from the story related by Swammerdam of bloody waters occurring at the Hague in 1760. One morning the town was in an uproar on finding the lakes and ditches full of blood, as they thought, which the night before was clear water. This depended upon prodigious swarms of red animals, known as water-fleas, *pulices arborescentes*, which were generated in a single night from their ova, lining the margins of the ditches and lakes. This occurrence is a very different thing from the genuine red rain, and does not in the least affect the main testimony.

Red Snow is no new phenomenon, for it was known to Aristotle, and probably seen by him, Humboldt thinks, in the mountains of Macedonia. In 1056 red snow fell in Armenia *(Math. Eretz)*. A shower of red snow fell at Pezzo, Valle Camonica, in March, 1803 *(Jour de Physique)*. A similar shower of red snow fell during three nights in March, 1808, in Carniola and neighbourhood, to the height of five feet ten inches. The earth was previously covered with snow of a pure white, and the coloured variety was again succeeded by the common sort, the two kinds remaining perfectly distinct, even during liquefaction. The red snow melted and evaporated, gave a little finely divided earth of a rose hue, consisting of silex, alumina, and oxide of iron. The same phenomenon was observed at the same time on the mountains of the Valteline, Brescia, and the Tyrol. Red rain and snow mingled with red dust, following thunder and lightning, fell at Gerace in Calabria, on March 14th, 1813. It was composed of silex, carbonate of lime, alumina, iron, and chrome. This red rain and snow fell in Tuscany, various parts of Calabria, and elsewhere. On April 15th, 1816, coloured snow again fell in Italy, particularly on Tonal and other mountains. It was brick red and left an earthy powder, very light and impalpable, unctuous to the touch, argillaceous odour, and sub-acid saline, and astringent taste. It was composed of silex, iron, alumina, &c. I am disposed to believe in these four instances of the present century, the colouring matter of the snow was due to volcanic ashes, known under the name of puzzolana, already referred to, resembling brick-dust, which view is favoured by the localities described.

Showers of red rain and red snow are therefore genuine and undoubted facts, and when we know what it is that imparts to them their peculiar colour, as has been fully explained, there is nothing preternatural or marvellous about them. Indeed, there is not a single phenomenon in nature, no matter how curious or uncommon, that connot be explained by the well known and unerring laws of natural and physical science.

Humboldt has remarked in his Cosmos, that although the existence of meteoric infusoria is more than doubtful, it cannot be denied that in the same manner as the pollen of the flowers of the pine is observed every year to fall from the atmosphere, minute infusorial animalcules may likewise be retained for a time in the strata of the air, after having been passively borne up by currents of aqueous vapour. In regard to this, Ehrenberg has discovered that the nebulous dust or sand which mariners often encounter in the vicinity of the Cape de Verde Islands, and even at a distance of 300 miles from the African shore, contains the remains of 18 species of silicious-shelled polygastric animalcules.

A shower of wheat is described as having occurred in Wiltshire : and a shower of millet seed in Silesia, mentioned in the *Ephem. Germanica.* They were most probably due to the effects of a hurricane, although this cannot be stated with certainty, as the original account we have not seen.

SHOWERS OF METEORITES OR METEORIC STONES.

These substances have long been objects of study and interest to the curious, and when occurring in a certain quantity are described as a shower of meteorites, although sometimes a single meteorite falls and becomes broken into numerous fragments, thus constituting the shower. In character they resemble ordinary stones, of a brownish colour, or metallic masses with a thin black crust, more or less shining. The one contains no iron, and the other does; this is well illustrated in the fine collection of these bodies preserved in the Mineralogical Gallery of the British Museum. Showers of meteorites have been known from the most ancient times, for both Livy and Pliny describe examples. Various accounts of them have appeared in modern times occurring in different parts of the world, too numerous to give in this place. Of single masses that have have fallen, the weight has varied from a few pounds to fifteen tons. One that fell in Brazil weighed upwards of 17,000 pounds ; another in Siberia 1680 pounds. One at Dhurmsalla, in India, in 1860, burst with a series of loud explosions, scattering the fragments to various distances over an extent of four miles : as other stones were found in more distant places, it is fair to infer that there was a shower of them. A shower of meteoric stones fell in Guernsey County, Ohio, on May 1st, 1860, at twenty minutes to one o'clock p.m. which was preceded by a clap of thunder, and an extra-ordinary sensation like an earthquake shock. This was observed for a distance of sixty miles ; many stones were seen to fall, and upwards of thirty were recovered. One weighed 51 pounds that had buried itself twenty inches in a stiff soil, and was so hot that it could be scarcely held in the hands. The others weighed 42, 36, and four pounds ; the heaviest was 103 pounds, and the lightest half-a-pound. All the stones were irregular in figure, and had the same general appearance, having a blackened smooth vitreous surface. Within, the stones had an ashy colour, with fine shining particles supposed to be nickel. My account of the meteoric shower is taken from Lieut. Tiddall, U.S. Army, in the local papers ; and Dr. Lawrence Smith, in *Amer. Jr. Science* for January, 1861. One hundred parts of the largest stone yielded ten of nickeliferous iron, and 89 of earthy minerals. The Guernsey shower has been compared to that which fell near L'Aigle, in France, on 26th April, 1812, at one o'clock p.m. A brilliant fiery globe burst with a loud explosion, followed by a great shower of meteoric stones to the number of 3000, the largest weighing over seventeen pounds. The direction of both of these showers was from S.E. to N.W. ; the extent of surface covered by the L'Aigle, $7\frac{1}{2}$ by $2\frac{1}{2}$ miles, and the Guernsey 10 by 3 miles; and both not only occurred about the same time of day, but were seen by a number of persons. A similar phenomenon occurred at Benares in 1798, followed by a shower of meteoric stones. There can be no doubt they are frequently happening over all parts of the globe, and those only are recorded that come within the knowledge of civilized communities. A great many must happen over the wide expanse of ocean that remain unknown.

To enter into a consideration of all the various theories to account for the occurrence of these meteorites would be a waste of time, and trying to the reader's patience. Laplace supposed them to be ejected from the Volcanoes of the Moon, a circumstance just as probable as that they should be formed in the atmosphere which others believe. The accepted doctrine, and clearly the correct one, is that they are cosmical bodies floating in space, and revolving round the sun in obedience to the laws of general gravity. If they meet the earth in their course and approach within the influence of its gravitation, they are immediately attracted to its surface and enter the atmosphere in a luminous condition, and fall in a strongly heated state. In all probability they may have been either thrown off from some planet into space, or they may be condensations of independent though small nebulous masses floating in space. That they are not of our earth is abundantly evident from their composition, as they are made up of certain minerals which are never met with in any other bodies. When a shower of several of them occurs, the inference is, that they have been floating together in company, through the influence of mutual attraction, and on coming within the sphere of terrestrial attraction have fallen together on the surface of the earth. Dr. Lawrence Smith, of Louisville, Kentucky, asserts that the light from meteoric stones, arises not from incandescence, but from electricity or some other cause. The noise attending their fall is due to concussion of the atmosphere and rapid motion through it, and partly to electrical discharge. And that the showers are not the results of fragments from the rupture of one solid body, but the separation of small and distinct aerolites that have entered our atmosphere in groups, as in two of the great showers already described.

The showers of luminous meteors seen in such profusion in 1868, do not come within the scope of this little work, as they have reference more to astronomy, and do not descend upon the earth, like other "Odd Showers."

SHOWERS OF OTHER BODIES.

Many substances occasionally descend in the form
of a shower, which cannot with propriety be classed
in the foregoing divisions, such as a gelatinous matter
falling in 1711 with a globe of fire in the Isle of
Lethy, in India. A shower of brimstone is mentioned by Warmius, which was most likely volcanic
in its origin.

If this little work meets with general approval, we
may on a future occasion enter more at length into the
various divisions which compose it. For the present
we simply describe what should be known and understood by every intelligent mind, whether among the
young or the old.

ODD SHOWERS.

In these pages, Showers Odd, form our theme
    That have existed from times remote ;
Truly marvellous do they seem
    To those who comprehend them not.

To such concerning frogs we don't give ear,
    Though well described by Pliny ;
Their reality though never proved, some aver,
    Whom the learned look upon as silly.

Of insects we have great abundance
    In the warm air of summer :
Ephemerae, shad-flies, mosquitoes, gnats ;
    With ants and locusts in large number.

But when we talk of showers of fishes,
    Perceptibly doth our visage lengthen ;
With good testimony it soon diminishes,
    From undoubted examples we make mention.

Ha ! Not so with newts and lizards,
  For we but a single instance give,
Yet if honest story be considered
  This odd shower we cannot disprove.

Showers of soot and sand, black, red, and white,
  Occur o'er seas and land of wide extent ;
Though from the heavens do they alight,
  Yet from earth's bowels mount the firmament.

What clouds are those on Afric's desert plains,
  That in the distance resemble ocean waves ?
Showers of sand which form the whirlwind's feast
  Alas, so fatal to Arab, and camel beast.

Showers of blood, red rain and snow,
  To our forefathers fatal omens, harbingers of evil,
With blood of butterflies, puzzolana of volcano,
  Vegetable organisms and infusorial animalcules.

The element of our bread, a shower of wheat,
  If true, from a hurricano fell ;
Yet not stranger than one of millet seed,
  On the authority of a learned Teuton, do we tell.

All these into insignificance fall,
　When we remember their rainy powers ;
Belong to our earth terrestrial,
　And thus are truly earthy showers.

But when we soar beyond our sphere,
　Do we encounter stones meteoric ;
Which revolve around the sun doth appear
　Until they approach our halo atmospheric.

Then with a devilish noise of thunder,
　Fiery flash, shake of earth and sense ;
A shower of meteorites excites our wonder,
　From an orange to a size immense.

Thus with showers odd are we inflicted,
　Not alone from earth, but the heavens,
Without an explanation clear imparted
　Would be like eating bread unleavened.

Though puzzling to the young, aye, and old,
　With nature's laws, are they simple,
Yet manifest the power of Almighty God,
　And love through Jesus for all his people.